Watching the Weather

Snow

Elizabeth Miles

Heinemann
LIBRARY

www.heinemann.co.uk/library

To order:
☎ Phone 44 (0) 1865 888066
🗎 Send a fax to 44 (0) 1865 314091
🖥 Visit the Heinemann Bookshop at www.heinemann.co.uk/library to browse our catalogue and order online.

First published in Great Britain by Heinemann Library, Halley Court, Jordan Hill, Oxford OX2 8EJ, part of Harcourt Education.
Heinemann is a registered trademark of Harcourt Education Ltd.

Editorial: Nancy Dickmann and Daniel Cuttell
Design: Richard Parker and Q2A Solutions
Illustrations: Jeff Edwards
Picture Research: Maria Joannou and Lynda Lines
Production: Camilla Smith

Originated by Ambassador Litho Ltd.
Printed and bound in China by South China Printing Company

ISBN 0 431 19036 4
09 08 07 06 05
10 9 8 7 6 5 4 3 2 1

British Library Cataloguing in Publication Data
Miles, Elizabeth
  Snow. – (Watching the weather)
  551.5'784

A full catalogue record for this book is available from the British Library.

Acknowledgements

The Publishers would like to thank the following for permission to reproduce photographs: Alamy pp. 12 (Bryan & Cherry Alexander), 20 (David Sanger), 21 (Chris Fredriksson); Corbis pp. 4 (Jose Luis Pelaez, Inc.), 5, 9 (Ariel Skelley), 16 (Tom Brakefield), 22 (Reuters), 24; FLPA p. 26; Getty Images pp. 7 (PhotoDisc), 8 (Taxi/Anne-Marie Webber), 10 (PhotoDisc), 13 (Image Bank/Kirk Anderson), 14 (Stone/John Marshall), 15 (Image Bank/Alan Majchrowicz), 17 (Stone/Daniel J. Cox), 18 (Image Bank/Mike Brinson); Reuters p. 23 (Paul Darrow); Science Photo Library p.25 (Mauro Fermariello); Still Pictures p. 27 (A. Riedmiller); Topham Picturepoint pp. 11 (Kent Meireis/The Image Works), 19; Tudor Photography pp. 28, 29.

Cover photograph of trees covered in snow in Washington, USA, reproduced with permission of Getty Images/The Image Bank.

The Publishers would like to thank Daniel Ogden for his assistance in the preparation of this book.

Every effort has been made to contact copyright holders of any material reproduced in this book. Any omissions will be rectified in subsequent printings if notice is given to the Publishers.

The paper used to print this book comes from sustainable resources.

Contents

Words appearing in the text in bold, **like this**, are explained in the Glossary.

 Find out more about snow at
www.heinemannexplore.co.uk

What is snow?

Snow is ice that falls from the sky as snowflakes. Lots of fallen snowflakes can cover the ground and other surfaces outside.

A covering of snow can make everything look white.

Sledges are fun to ride over the snow.

After a snowfall, the snow can **melt** or stay in a layer on the ground. Sometimes the snow stays and another snowfall makes the snow thicker.

Where does snow come from?

Snow is made up of tiny bits of ice called **ice crystals**. The ice crystals grow from **water vapour** in cold clouds.

Snowflakes are six-sided shapes made of ice crystals.

The ice cystals
bump into each other

The ice crystals
make snowflakes

Water in the air
(water vapour)
freezes into ice crystals

The ice crystals in clouds bump
into each other and stick together
to make snowflakes. Every snowflake
looks a bit different.

Snowflakes

Snowflakes can be small or large, hard or soft. Snowflakes often **melt** on their way down from the clouds and reach the ground as raindrops.

Large snowflakes can be made up of hundreds of **ice crystals**.

Small snowflakes can be very powdery and will not stick together.

Small, hard snowflakes can sting your face in the wind. Large, soft snowflakes look fluffy. Some snowflakes stick together easily so you can make snowmen or snowballs.

When does it snow?

Snow usually falls in winter. In the winter the air and ground are often very cold. Fallen snow stays while it is cold and **melts** when it gets warmer.

Skiing on snow is a popular sport in the winter.

When fallen snow melts, it changes. First, it melts into **slush**, then water, and drains away or dries up. This can take a few days or several weeks.

In the summer, the snow melts and people can enjoy walking and cycling instead of skiing.

Snow around the world

Places like hot deserts and the **tropical regions** have no snow all year. The weather is too hot for snow. Other places have snowfalls throughout the year.

In the cold **Arctic**, snow covers the ground for most of the year.

As you climb a high mountain it often gets colder. Near the top there may be snow.

The tops of mountains can have snow all year round. This is because the air is very cold high up. The place where this snow starts is called the snowline.

Snow and plants

Many plants grow and flower in the winter snow. A layer of snow can be like a blanket. It covers plants and keeps them warm.

These winter flowers are called snowdrops.

Fir trees grow on mountain slopes where there is lots of snow. Layers of snow can be heavy and can break tree branches. Fir trees have a special shape to stop this.

Heavy snow will slide off the sloping branches of fir trees.

Snow and animals

Many animals can live in places where there is lots of snow. The snowshoe hare has extra large, very furry paws for hopping across the snow.

The snowshoe hare's big feet stop it from sinking into soft, deep snow.

The Arctic fox's white coat is difficult to see against the white snow.

The Arctic fox's brown coat turns white in winter. This means that **predators** cannot see it easily. Its winter fur is woolly and warm, too.

Snow and people

Snow can be great fun. As fallen snow squashes together it becomes firm packed snow. This firm snow is good for skiing, snowboarding and other sports.

Snow boarders can slide very fast on firm snow.

Some people wear snowshoes to stop them from sinking into deep snow.

It is important to keep our bodies warm in snowy weather. We must wear warm clothes and keep moving about.

Staying safe

Snowy weather can be dangerous. When bright sunlight bounces off snow it can hurt our eyes. It is important to wear sunglasses.

Mountain climbers wear sunglasses to protect their eyes from sunshine bouncing off the snow.

Cars can slide about in the snow. Driving too fast in snow can cause an accident. Sometimes car wheels get stuck in thick snow.

Some people put chains on their car wheels. These help grip the snow.

Snowstorms

A blizzard is a winter snowstorm. Strong winds blow and lots of snow falls quickly. It is difficult to see anything in a blizzard.

Snow ploughs try to keep main roads clear during blizzards.

The wind may blow the falling snow into piles, called snowdrifts. Snowdrifts can cover cars and trains so that the people inside have to be rescued.

A snowdrift can be as high as a house.

Disaster: avalanche

An avalanche is when a lot of snow suddenly crashes down a mountainside. Lots of things can set off an avalanche, such as a thick layer of new snow.

An avalanche can fall down a mountainside as fast as a car.

Trained dogs use their sense of smell to find people buried in an avalanche.

The heavy snow in an avalanche can damage houses. It can bury people, and even whole villages. There is little warning so people cannot always get away.

Is it snow?

An icy white covering might be **frost** and not snow. Frost does not fall from clouds as snowflakes. It forms from **water vapour** in the air close to the ground.

Frost can cover the ground and objects outside. It can look just like snow.

Pretend snow is sometimes sprayed on ski slopes if no real snow has fallen.

People make pretend snow. It is used to make winter scenes in films and on television. Pretend snow can be made from ice, paper, plastic, **foam** or **chemicals**.

Project: how to measure snow

Now you know how snow is made, you can find out how much frozen water there is in snow.

You will need:
- a straight-sided glass jar
- a ruler
- cardboard
- snow

1. Find a flat layer of snow outside and measure its depth with a ruler.

2. Hold the jar upside-down. Push it down through the snow into the ground.

3. Slide the cardboard underneath so that you gather the snow in the jar.

4. Let the snow in the jar **melt**. Measure the depth of the water left in the jar.

5. Compare the snow measurement with the water measurement.

Why is the snow deeper than the melted water? It is because there is lots of air trapped in the snow, making it thicker.

Glossary

Arctic very cold area around the North Pole

chemicals chemicals are used by scientists to make all kinds of things, like medicines

foam white froth, like lots of soap bubbles

freeze turn into a very cold solid (water freezes into ice)

frost frozen water vapour close to the ground

ice crystal very tiny bit of frozen water

melt change from a solid to a liquid (ice melts into water)

predator animal that hunts another animal for food

slush mix of ice and water

snow plough machine with big blades for pushing thick snow off roads

tropical region part of the Earth where the weather is hot and wet

water vapour water in the air. Water vapour is a gas that we cannot see

Find out more

More books to read

Looking at Animals in Cold Places, Moira Butterfield (Raintree, 2000)

Science of Weather: Snow and the Earth, Nikki Bundey (Carolrhoda Books, 2001)

What is Weather?: Snow, Miranda Ashwell and Andy Owen (Heinemann Library, 2002)

Websites to visit

http://www.bbc.co.uk/weather/weatherwise
A website packed with information about how the weather affects us, weather images and facts, and lots of fun games, projects and activities.

http://www.snow-forecast.com
Lots of snow pictures and snow forecasts from around the world.

Index

Titles in the *Watching the Weather* series include:

Hardback   0 431 19022 4

Hardback   0 431 19023 2

Hardback   0 431 19024 0

Hardback   0 431 19025 9

Hardback   0 431 19026 7

Hardback   0 431 19035 6

Hardback   0 431 19036 4

Hardback   0 431 19037 2

Hardback   0 431 19034 8

Find out about the other titles in this series on our website www.heinemann.co.uk/library